I dedicate this book to me - the me as I stand Today (Badass), to the little me who still resides within me (who struggled but is still healing every day), and to the future me that because of this book I continue write, manifest and rise up as the S-Hero of my own Story!

I dedicate this book to YOU. For having listened to the Whisper that said, "Give this journal a chance" and to the little YOU that resides in you that seeks guidance, silence, stillness, healing and connection with self and source.

I dedicate this book to my ancestors and to the great sages that lived before you and me who passed this information to all of us. I dedicate this book to Divine Source (God, Hashem, The Great Mystery or Great Mother) for the inspiration to write this book and create all the offerings I have produced and is yet to come.

Welcome!

Thank you for taking an active approach to your meditation practice. So many people want to start a regular practice and don't know where to begin.

I have made it easy for you. Place the book where you plan to sit for meditation daily.

Do your morning, evening and weekly check ins. This journal will guide you along your journey and help you cultivate a regular meditation practice. Give it an honest 30 days. If you miss a day, that is OK too. Just recommit and sit for your next scheduled meditation. The journal will also expose you to various meditation techniques and reflections offered to give you a well rounded, non-denominational, experience and to help you grow your practice. Use the ones that resonate. Leave the rest behind.

For those of you who are just beginning., my suggestion is you start with 5-8 minutes and every 3 days, increase your sitting 2-3 minutes until you are able to comfortably sit for 15-30 minutes. No one is perfect at meditating. No sitting is the same, either. Lean into it. Give it time. Remember, the key to success is not about perfect but about effort. Five minutes is better than nothing. Listen to the whispers. You will find that the more you do it, the more it will truly get out of this daily practice. I would love your feedback! Stay connected!

Peace & Silence * Erica Garcia Abergel

Initial Wellness check in

DATE _____

HOW DOES YOUR BODY FEEL TODAY & OVERALL?

_____

WHAT WOULD YOU LIKE TO ACHIEVE FROM THESE NEXT 30 DAYS?

○ _____

○ _____

○ _____

○ _____

ARE YOU IN BALANCE?

MARK IF YOU FEEL ANY PAIN

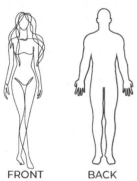

FRONT   BACK

3 AREAS I NEED TO FOCUS ON

○ _____

○ _____

○ _____

WHICH EMOTIONS ARE CURRENTLY PREDOMINANT?

_____

MENTAL OUTLOOK - HOW INSPIRED DO YOU FEEL?

Weekly Focus

M

T

W

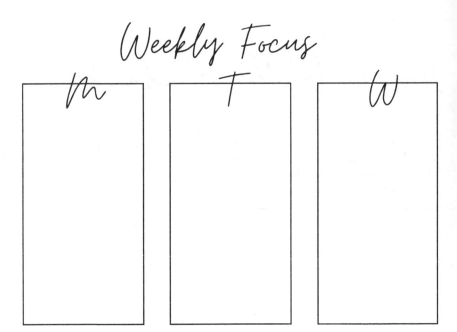

WEEKLY AFFIRMATION, REFLECTION OR FOCUS

HABITS & RITUALS

Journaled ○ ○ ○ ○ ○ ○ ○
Connected / Prayed ○ ○ ○ ○ ○ ○ ○
Visualized / Goals ○ ○ ○ ○ ○ ○ ○
Meditation / Breathe ○ ○ ○ ○ ○ ○ ○
Yoga ○ ○ ○ ○ ○ ○ ○
Organize Space/Life ○ ○ ○ ○ ○ ○ ○
Self-Care ○ ○ ○ ○ ○ ○ ○
Played/ was Creative ○ ○ ○ ○ ○ ○ ○
Cooked/Ate Healthy ○ ○ ○ ○ ○ ○ ○
Moved / Exercised ○ ○ ○ ○ ○ ○ ○
Was out in Nature ○ ○ ○ ○ ○ ○ ○
Met a friend/Family ○ ○ ○ ○ ○ ○ ○
Served Community ○ ○ ○ ○ ○ ○ ○
Digital Detox ○ ○ ○ ○ ○ ○ ○

MUST DO LIST

○ _____
○ _____
○ _____

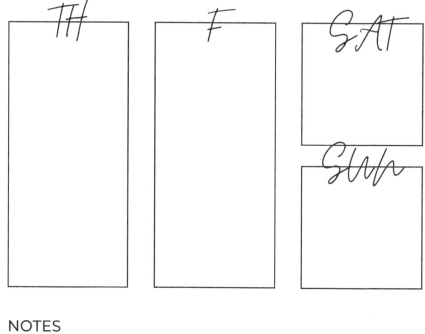

TH

F

SAT

SUN

NOTES

Day 1

The simple set up - Ideally you will also face in the direction of the East. Find a comfortable seated position. You want to be able to sit comfortably for the duration.
Place your hands on your thighs - palms up or down. Relax and begin to breath in and out with your nose. Scan your body from bottom to top with your breath and with each exhale try to relax and release the tension.
Set your timer for 10 minutes. This may or may not be your first seated meditation but it is good to set the timer simply as a beginning baseline to see how your practice has grown at the end of these 30 days. Nothing sets the mind ready for meditation is better than as you settle in, take a few moments to ask yourself the simple questions.

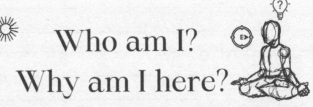

Who am I?
Why am I here?

Use those questions as your mantra (repeated affirmation).

PRE-MEDITATION - MIND DUMP -
3 MINUTE JOURNALING

Daily

Morning

Meditation

_____
_____
_____
_____

_____
_____
_____
_____
_____

DURATION & TYPE OF MEDITATION
○ _____
○ _____
○ _____

WHAT INSPIRED YOU THE MOST TODAY? MANTRA USED OR REFLECTIONS

WHAT EMOTIONS HAVE YOU FELT TODAY?

OTHER EXPERIENCES & OBSERVATIONS
○ _____
○ _____
○ _____

HOW WOULD YOU RATE THE SESSIION?

☆ ☆ ☆ ☆ ☆

Evening Meditation

For your second meditation, take a few minutes to quickly recap your day from the moment you woke up to the present moment. Replay the day - interactions and decisions. Don't get stuck. Practice acknowledgement and non-attachment. Observe. Take in the lesson and make a mental note on how you would have handled differently. Let it all go in peace.

TODAY I LEARNED....

_____

_____

_____

_____

I AM GRATEFUL FOR...

_____

_____

_____

_____

I GO TO BED FEELING...

_____

_____

_____

_____

TOMORROW I WISH TO...

_____

_____

_____

_____

Day 2

Today, try to just stay aware of the rhythm of your breath.
You may start with a 5 count box breath - Count to 5 as you
inhale, then gently hold the breath at the top of the inhale for
a count of 5, then exhale for a 5 count. Lastly, keep the lungs
empty for a 5 count before you inhale again.

Try this pranayama (breath practice) for about 5-7 rounds
before you settle into your natural breath. You may have
found that the mental counting was in and of itself a mantra
and bringing you to the present moment. As you begin
becoming more aware of the breath some people can also
begin to notice sensations in their body. Many of us have
become so desensitized and disconnected that we forgot how
to tap into this awareness. Some people find it helpful to
place their left hand on their belly and right hand on their
hearts. It can be very soothing. You can give it a try. Notice
the lungs as they expand with each inhale. Notice how the
body collapses within on the exhales. Can you ride the wave
of the inhale and notice the exhale breath.

Practice awareness with non-attachment. That's it. This is your
meditation today. Nothing more nothing less. Just connecting but
to observe anything that comes up in your body or mind and
journal it. This will be helpful to start intentionally monitoring
your growth in your practice.

PRE-MEDITATION - MIND DUMP - 3 MINUTE JOURNALING

Daily

Morning

Meditation

_____

_____

_____

_____

_____

_____

_____

_____

_____

DURATION & TYPE OF MEDITATION

○ _____

○ _____

○ _____

WHAT EMOTIONS HAVE YOU FELT TODAY?

HOW WOULD YOU RATE THE SESSIION?

☆ ☆ ☆ ☆ ☆

WHAT INSPIRED YOU THE MOST TODAY? MANTRA USED OR REFLECTIONS

OTHER EXPERIENCES & OBSERVATIONS

○ _____

○ _____

○ _____

Evening Meditation

For your second meditation, take a few minutes to quickly recap your day from the moment you woke up to the present moment. Replay the day - interactions and decisions. Don't get stuck. Practice acknowledgement and non-attachment. Observe. Take in the lesson and make a mental note on how you would have handled differently. Let it all go in peace.

TODAY I LEARNED....

_____

_____

_____

_____

I AM GRATFUL FOR...

_____

_____

_____

_____

I GO TO BED FEELING...

_____

_____

_____

_____

TOMORROW I WISH TO...

_____

_____

_____

_____

Day 3

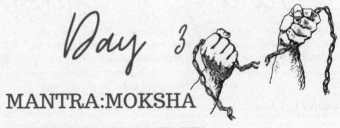

MANTRA:MOKSHA

"I AM EMOTIONALLY FREE"
I AM GOING TO.......
I CAN ......
I WILL ......
I AM FREE FROM ......
I RELEASE.. AND CALL IN THE NEW
ENERGY OF...

Let us break the chains that bind us. It takes an open heart and mind to recognize where we are being held behind. What are our limiting beliefs? Where are we being emotionally hijacked? What mistakes do you keep repeating? It courage to lean into this discomfort. You can do it. Moksha is said to liberate the soul freeing and heal you from emotional pain and also the courage to face your fears of the future. Envision yourself breaking out of these shackles and start bringing in the energy of the opposite you seek as stated above.

NOTE: Why chant in the Sanskrit language? Well, it is important that you understand that Sanskrit has 49 letters and 35 have a soft, vibrational aspect to them. Therefore, it is said that when one recites 'Mantra,' taken from the root words "manas" (the linear thinking mind) and "tra" (to cross over) what we are doing is crossing over between the embodied physical body to our energetic and spiritual bodies. When you compare repeating mantra, similar to a chorus line in your favorite song, you understand it's ability to transport you to 'another place in time.' There is power in the repetition of mantra. Yes, you can repeat in your minds but you will notice there is more vibration when chanted out loud a few times before you settle into your silent practice. Mantra can take us beyond our physical to deep states of energetic consciousness that can be truly healing, and liberating as it touches our hearts and souls. I give you the English translations but I encourage you to try to meditate in their originally intended Sanskrit Mantra for the full benefits.

PRE-MEDITATION - MIND DUMP - 3 MINUTE JOURNALING

Daily

Morning

Meditation

_____

_____

_____

_____

_____

_____

_____

_____

_____

_____

_____

DURATION & TYPE OF MEDITATION

○ _____

○ _____

○ _____

WHAT INSPIRED YOU THE MOST TODAY? MANTRA USED OR REFLECTIONS

WHAT EMOTIONS HAVE YOU FELT TODAY?

OTHER EXPERIENCES & OBSERVATIONS

HOW WOULD YOU RATE THE SESSIION?

☆ ☆ ☆ ☆ ☆

○ _____

○ _____

○ _____

Evening Meditation

For your second meditation, take a few minutes to quickly recap your day from the moment you woke up to the present moment. Replay the day - interactions and decisions. Don't get stuck. Practice acknowledgement and non-attachment. Observe. Take in the lesson and make a mental note on how you would have handled differently. Let it all go in peace.

TODAY I LEARNED....

_____

_____

_____

_____

I AM GRATFUL FOR...

_____

_____

_____

_____

I GO TO BED FEELING...

_____

_____

_____

_____

TOMORROW I WISH TO...

_____

_____

_____

_____

Day 4

MANTRA: AHIMSA (Non-Violence)

"I AM COMMITTED TO NON-VIOLENCE. I AM BRINGING IN MORE LOVE AND COMPASSION INTO MY LIFE. I AM PEACE. I GIVE LOVE."

MANTRA: LOKAH SAMASTA SUKHINO BHAVANTU

"May all beings everywhere be happy and free, and may the thoughts, words, and actions of my own life contribute in some way to that happiness, peace, ease and the freedom for all.

This mantra takes you out of your own mind from personal, self thoughts and more into the head space of sending out the energy of peace and love and recognizing how our actions are all interconnected to all beings in the world. It is the sending out of positive energy to the world.

Lokah: location, realm, all universes that is in existence now;

Samastah: all the beings sharing that same location;

Sukhino: energy centered in happiness and joy, freedom from suffering;

Bhav: the divine state of unified connectedness and existence; and

Antu: "may it be so" or "it must be so," (when "antu" is used as an ending to mantras, it transforms the mantra into a powerful pledge).

PRE-MEDITATION - MIND DUMP - 3 MINUTE JOURNALING

Daily

Morning

Meditation

_____
_____
_____
_____
_____
_____

_____
_____
_____
_____

DURATION & TYPE OF MEDITATION

○ _____
○ _____
○ _____

WHAT EMOTIONS HAVE YOU FELT TODAY?

HOW WOULD YOU RATE THE SESSIION?

☆ ☆ ☆ ☆ ☆

WHAT INSPIRED YOU THE MOST TODAY? MANTRA USED OR REFLECTIONS

OTHER EXPERIENCES & OBSERVATIONS

○ _____
○ _____
○ _____

Evening Meditation

For your second meditation, take a few minutes to quickly recap your day from the moment you woke up to the present moment. Replay the day - interactions and decisions. Don't get stuck. Practice acknowledgement and non-attachment. Observe. Take in the lesson and make a mental note on how you would have handled differently. Let it all go in peace.

TODAY I LEARNED....

_____

_____

_____

_____

I AM GRATFUL FOR...

_____

_____

_____

_____

I GO TO BED FEELING...

_____

_____

_____

_____

TOMORROW I WISH TO...

_____

_____

_____

_____

Day 5

MANTRA: SA TA NA MA

This is the classic Kundalini , also known as Kirtan
Kriya. There are many benefits to it. Basically, it
balances out your excess emotions and brings in the
energy of balance. We each have a Sun (our right side
of our body) and Moon/THA (our left side of our body)
energy. It said that it balances the left and right
hemispheres of the brain, our HA/THA energies and
even increases our intuition. It has a very calming
effect too. So, I personally love to do it often to start
my day or during times of high stress when I just need a
quick 5 minute reset in my mind and emotions.

MOVING HAND MUDRA FOR THIS MEDITATION:
You will lightly move with each syllable touching the
thumb to the tips of each finger as you chant.
SA = thumb to pointer finger
TA = thumb to middle finger
NA = thumb to ring finger
MA = thumb to pinky finger

PRE-MEDITATION - MIND DUMP - 3 MINUTE JOURNALING

Daily

Morning

Meditation

_____

_____

_____

_____

_____

_____

_____

_____

_____

_____

DURATION & TYPE OF MEDITATION

○ _____

○ _____

○ _____

WHAT INSPIRED YOU THE MOST TODAY? MANTRA USED OR REFLECTIONS

WHAT EMOTIONS HAVE YOU FELT TODAY?

HOW WOULD YOU RATE THE SESSIION?

☆ ☆ ☆ ☆ ☆

OTHER EXPERIENCES & OBSERVATIONS

○ _____

○ _____

○ _____

Evening Meditation

For your second meditation, take a few minutes to quickly recap your day from the moment you woke up to the present moment. Replay the day - interactions and decisions. Don't get stuck. Practice acknowledgement and non-attachment. Observe. Take in the lesson and make a mental note on how you would have handled differently. Let it all go in peace.

TODAY I LEARNED....

_____

_____

_____

_____

I AM GRATFUL FOR...

_____

_____

_____

_____

I GO TO BED FEELING...

_____

_____

_____

_____

TOMORROW I WISH TO...

_____

_____

_____

_____

Day 6

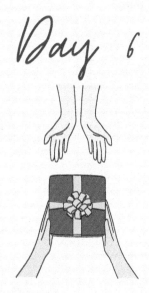

MANTRA: KLEEM

"I am fully open to give and receive love. I accept and receive an overwhelming overflow of abundance in my life. New opportunities are coming to me and I am open and willing to receive them. I am calling in my desires for...... and I am commanding the universe to to bring it to me or better."

TO CHANT "KLEEM," You MUST to chant it 108X in a row. I like to use a Japa Mala to keep the count. You can chant out loud or to yourself. The key is to draw out the "E," as in "KLEEEEEEEM." Move the mantra with your breath. Kleem is said to draw in the energy of irresistible attraction in all areas of our lives - money, love, abundance, beauty and nature.

PRE-MEDITATION - MIND DUMP - 3 MINUTE JOURNALING

Daily

Morning

Meditation

_____

_____

_____

_____

_____

_____

_____

_____

_____

_____

DURATION & TYPE OF MEDITATION

○ _____

○ _____

○ _____

WHAT INSPIRED YOU THE MOST TODAY? MANTRA USED OR REFLECTIONS

WHAT EMOTIONS HAVE YOU FELT TODAY?

HOW WOULD YOU RATE THE SESSIION?

☆ ☆ ☆ ☆ ☆

OTHER EXPERIENCES & OBSERVATIONS

○ _____

○ _____

○ _____

Evening Meditation

For your second meditation, take a few minutes to quickly recap your day from the moment you woke up to the present moment. Replay the day - interactions and decisions. Don't get stuck. Practice acknowledgement and non-attachment. Observe. Take in the lesson and make a mental note on how you would have handled differently. Let it all go in peace.

TODAY I LEARNED....

_____

_____

_____

_____

I AM GRATFUL FOR...

_____

_____

_____

_____

I GO TO BED FEELING...

_____

_____

_____

_____

TOMORROW I WISH TO...

_____

_____

_____

_____

Day 7

MANTRA: Om AH Hum
(some prefer HUNG)

OM AH HUM(HUNG) is a mantra that brings a lot of vibrations to the heart center. It chanted out loud and chanted to provide for purity and clarity of the Mind, to purify your Speech, and purify and detoxify the Body. You can use either HUM or HUNG. So, use the one that resonates with you. It is often activated in the body from the Crown of the head, traveling down through the third eye center, to the throat, and down into the heart. This one is a Buddhist mantra so you will also notice the colors of the areas are different than what most people classically know as the 7 main chakra colors. Work with this color combination as you, in your minds eye envision them in your own body as you activate them with each word. Give it your full concentration. Chant with the natural rhythm of your breath. Envision the white light at the top of the head as you inhale and chant OM. Pull the energy out and invigorate the light energy between the brow line. Then as you drop down and begin to exhale into the AH vibration feel it drop and concentrate on the throat area providing for the speech. Project the vibration outward with that glowing red light energy. On the end of that exhale the remainder of the breath and deeply vibrate the word HUM. Being sure to close the lips and feel the vibrations of the drawn out "mmm" from the throat dropping deeply into the heart center. Imagine the dark blue light getting bigger and bigger covering your heart and torso.

Weekly Wellness check in

DATE _____

HOW DOES YOUR BODY FEEL
TODAY? DID YOU MOVE THIS
WEEK? HOW WAS YOUR DIET?

WHAT FELT GOOD THIS WEEK?

○ _____
○ _____
○ _____
○ _____

ARE YOU IN BALANCE?

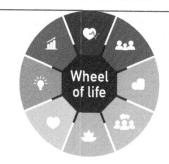

MARK IF YOU FEEL ANY PAIN

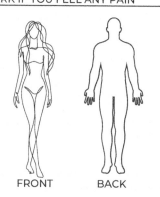

FRONT   BACK

3 AREAS I NEED TO FOCUS ON

○ _____
○ _____
○ _____

WHICH EMOTIONS WERE
PREDOMINANT THIS WEEK?

MENTAL OUTLOOK - HOW
INSPIRED WERE YOU THIS WEEK?

PRE-MEDITATION - MIND DUMP - 3 MINUTE JOURNALING

Daily

Morning

Meditation

_____

_____

_____

_____

_____

_____

_____

_____

_____

DURATION & TYPE OF MEDITATION

○ _____

○ _____

○ _____

WHAT INSPIRED YOU THE MOST TODAY? MANTRA USED OR REFLECTIONS

WHAT EMOTIONS HAVE YOU FELT TODAY?

OTHER EXPERIENCES & OBSERVATIONS

○ _____

○ _____

○ _____

HOW WOULD YOU RATE THE SESSIION?

☆ ☆ ☆ ☆ ☆

Evening Meditation

For your second meditation, take a few minutes to quickly recap your day from the moment you woke up to the present moment. Replay the day - interactions and decisions. Don't get stuck. Practice acknowledgement and non-attachment. Observe. Take in the lesson and make a mental note on how you would have handled differently. Let it all go in peace.

TODAY I LEARNED....

_____

_____

_____

_____

I AM GRATEFUL FOR...

_____

_____

_____

_____

I GO TO BED FEELING...

_____

_____

_____

_____

TOMORROW I WISH TO...

_____

_____

_____

_____

Weekly Meditation check in

DATE _____

TOP 3 THINGS I DID THIS WEEK

○ _____

○ _____

○ _____

MOST REWARDING INTERACTION I HAD THIS WEEK

THIS WEEK I FELT

THIS WEEK I NOTICED A SHIFT IN...

_____

_____

_____

_____

NEXT WEEK I WANT TO...

WHAT WAS MY FAVORITE REFLECTION THIS WEEK?

MY RANKING OF THE WEEK

☆ ☆ ☆ ☆ ☆

Day 8

PRAYER AS MANTRA

Lord, where will you guide me today? Today, I lean not unto my own understanding but for what you have planned for my life. Open all of my eyes. Let me see what I need to see. Let me leave the ego behind and humbly walk where you are taking me. Whatever is thy will, it is my will to do it. I will remain open to listening with my eyes, ears, and heart. May I see your signs everywhere guiding me and answering my prayers.

This is to show you that you can set out a prayer and then sit in stillness.
Today's prayer was inspired by
Psalm 119:18
"Let me see clearly so that I may take in the amazing things coming from Your law."

It is not only a surrendering to that which is greater than us but also a pledge that we will be obedient and allow ourselves to be lead. Oftentimes we ask for something but when we don't get it in the container we were expecting, we resist it. Don't be stubborn. Forget about what you want and accept what will be according to your life design. Focus on the end result you seek and allow the natural path of law of attraction to get you there (if meant to be).

Weekly Focus

M

T

W

MUST DO LIST

○ _____
○ _____
○ _____

HABITS & RITUALS

Journaled	○	○	○	○	○	○
Connected / Prayed	○	○	○	○	○	○
Visualized / Goals	○	○	○	○	○	○
Meditation / Breathe	○	○	○	○	○	○
Yoga	○	○	○	○	○	○
Organize Space/Life	○	○	○	○	○	○
Self-Care	○	○	○	○	○	○
Played/ was Creative	○	○	○	○	○	○
Cooked/Ate Healthy	○	○	○	○	○	○
Moved / Exercised	○	○	○	○	○	○
Was out in Nature	○	○	○	○	○	○
Met a friend/Family	○	○	○	○	○	○
Served Community	○	○	○	○	○	○
Digital Detox	○	○	○	○	○	○

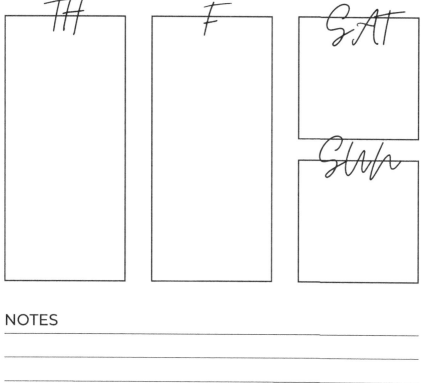

TH

F

SAT

SUN

NOTES

PRE-MEDITATION - MIND DUMP - 3 MINUTE JOURNALING

Daily

Morning

Meditation

_____

_____

_____

_____

_____

_____

_____

_____

_____

DURATION & TYPE OF MEDITATION

○ _____

○ _____

○ _____

WHAT INSPIRED YOU THE MOST TODAY? MANTRA USED OR REFLECTIONS

WHAT EMOTIONS HAVE YOU FELT TODAY?

HOW WOULD YOU RATE THE SESSIION?

☆ ☆ ☆ ☆ ☆

OTHER EXPERIENCES & OBSERVATIONS

○ _____

○ _____

○ _____

Evening Meditation

For your second meditation, take a few minutes to quickly recap your day from the moment you woke up to the present moment. Replay the day - interactions and decisions. Don't get stuck. Practice acknowledgement and non-attachment. Observe. Take in the lesson and make a mental note on how you would have handled differently. Let it all go in peace.

TODAY I LEARNED....

_____
_____
_____
_____

I AM GRATFUL FOR...

_____
_____
_____
_____

I GO TO BED FEELING...

_____
_____
_____
_____

TOMORROW I WISH TO...

_____
_____
_____
_____

Day 9

MANTRA: AGNI MEELE PUROHITAM "I SURRENDER TO THE FIRE OF TRANSFORMATION"

LET'S TALK ABOUT MANIFESTING DREAMS AND SENDING NOTES TO THE UNIVERSE.

There are many different cultures that have various beliefs and respect for the power of the moon. Just as the sun circles us, so does the moon. This really isn't witchery. It is more about using the power of law and attraction, cleansing and letting go. When you burn a letter it can be very cathartic. It is a "so it shall be" energy. You can offer forgiveness and finally let go or you can say, "Hey, Universe... shift what needs to be shifted... bring me my desires!". Remember there is power and energy in words. It is even more powerful when you write down (not type) your dreams, goals and releases. Fire does have the power of transformation. So, transform that energy. Give it a try and decide what you want to write and send it up to the universe!

MORE TIPS: Want more bang for your buck? CHECK OUT THE MOON PHASE you are in.

It is generally thought that you RELEASE from when the time period between the Full Moon to the next New Moon and you MANIFEST from when it is a New Moon until the next Full Moon.

PRE-MEDITATION - MIND DUMP - 3 MINUTE JOURNALING

Daily

Morning

Meditation

DURATION & TYPE OF MEDITATION

○ _____

○ _____

○ _____

WHAT INSPIRED YOU THE MOST TODAY? MANTRA USED OR REFLECTIONS

WHAT EMOTIONS HAVE YOU FELT TODAY?

HOW WOULD YOU RATE THE SESSIION?

☆ ☆ ☆ ☆ ☆

OTHER EXPERIENCES & OBSERVATIONS

○ _____

○ _____

○ _____

Evening Meditation

For your second meditation, take a few minutes to quickly recap your day from the moment you woke up to the present moment. Replay the day - interactions and decisions. Don't get stuck. Practice acknowledgement and non-attachment. Observe. Take in the lesson and make a mental note on how you would have handled differently. Let it all go in peace.

TODAY I LEARNED....

_____
_____
_____
_____

I AM GRATFUL FOR...

_____
_____
_____
_____

I GO TO BED FEELING...

_____
_____
_____
_____

TOMORROW I WISH TO...

_____
_____
_____
_____

Day 10

MANTRA: OM MANI PADME HUM

We see these symbols and prayer flags everywhere & never knew the meaning. As explained earlier of the importance of chanting in Sanskrit, one should always be sensing the vibrations but also really be thinking of the meaning of what you are chanting. For this one, "Om Mani Padme Hum," the translation is literally "Praise to the Jewel in the Lotus."

It is suggested you sit comfortably in a meditative state, focus on your breath, turn your attention inward, begin on your inhale & repeat it 21 or 108 times with a calm, focused and meditative mind..

It is said you should not seek the Buddha outside of you but rather within. This mantra has deep meaning & a path in which an indivisible can unite method with wisdom.

OM= represents divine sound composed of three letters. A, U, and M. These symbolize the pure exalted body, speech, and mind. It brings in more connectedness to source and generosity while purifying one from false ego.

MANI= The Illusion, "Jewel." Symbolizes the altruistic intention to become enlightened, compassion, & the essence of love. Rooted from "Ma" representing your ethics or morals purifying you from jealousy. The "Ni" representing patience while one is in the pursuit of their passion.

PADME = Lotus which symbolizes light & wisdom. Just as a lotus grows forth from mud it is also sullied by the faults & debris of mud. The "Pad" represents your diligence to purify from ignorance. While the "Me" helps with renunciation from greed.

There is wisdom and purity can be realized when one recognizes impermanence and stays open to the messages and flow of life & the universe.

HUM= Indivisibility and union. This wisdom helps us to purify us from aggression.

In terms of the seed syllables, one can see how reciting this mantra can truly bring about wisdom and tenacity. One will become more purified and undisturbed from outside sources

PRE-MEDITATION - MIND DUMP - 3 MINUTE JOURNALING

Daily

Morning

Meditation

_____

_____

_____

_____

_____

_____

_____

_____

_____

DURATION & TYPE OF MEDITATION

○ _____

○ _____

○ _____

WHAT INSPIRED YOU THE MOST TODAY? MANTRA USED OR REFLECTIONS

WHAT EMOTIONS HAVE YOU FELT TODAY?

OTHER EXPERIENCES & OBSERVATIONS

○ _____

○ _____

○ _____

HOW WOULD YOU RATE THE SESSIION?

☆ ☆ ☆ ☆ ☆

Evening Meditation

For your second meditation, take a few minutes to quickly recap your day from the moment you woke up to the present moment. Replay the day - interactions and decisions. Don't get stuck. Practice acknowledgement and non-attachment. Observe. Take in the lesson and make a mental note on how you would have handled differently. Let it all go in peace.

TODAY I LEARNED....

_____
_____
_____
_____

I AM GRATFUL FOR...

_____
_____
_____
_____

I GO TO BED FEELING...

_____
_____
_____
_____

TOMORROW I WISH TO...

_____
_____
_____
_____

Day 11

MANTRA: NETI-NETI
"Not this, Nor this"

What am I feeling? What are the thoughts that are racing in my head? The negative judgments and labels? How do I feel? Why is my mind ruminating over and over? Can I let it go? Can I calm the chaos in my head and move beyond these false impression in my mind and ego and realize who I really am? "I" am NOT these labels (stupid, lazy), titles (jobs), thoughts, roles (parent, sibling, friend, child) or feelings. Neti-Neti... I am beyond all of these things.

Neti-Neti is a simple yet powerful mantra. It is said to be over 8,000 years old stemming from the Jnana yoga and Advaita Vedanta teachings. It helps you move past the delusional sense (anatman) of self and feel connected to what is real (atman).

Use Neti-Neti during times where you find yourself in need of calming the mind, reduce your stress, feeling where your thoughts are taking over or as you are asking yourself the contemplative questions such as, "Who am I? Why am I here? What makes my heart happy? What am I grateful for? What do I know to be true in my physical, emotional, material, relationship and spiritual realms?
Invite in the stillness so the true answers can come in.

PRE-MEDITATION - MIND DUMP - 3 MINUTE JOURNALING

Daily

Morning

Meditation

_____

_____

_____

_____

_____

_____

_____

_____

_____

_____

_____

DURATION & TYPE OF MEDITATION

○ _____

○ _____

○ _____

WHAT INSPIRED YOU THE MOST TODAY? MANTRA USED OR REFLECTIONS

WHAT EMOTIONS HAVE YOU FELT TODAY?

OTHER EXPERIENCES & OBSERVATIONS

○ _____

○ _____

○ _____

HOW WOULD YOU RATE THE SESSIION?

☆ ☆ ☆ ☆ ☆

Evening Meditation

For your second meditation, take a few minutes to quickly recap your day from the moment you woke up to the present moment. Replay the day - interactions and decisions. Don't get stuck. Practice acknowledgement and non-attachment. Observe. Take in the lesson and make a mental note on how you would have handled differently. Let it all go in peace.

TODAY I LEARNED....

_____

_____

_____

_____

I AM GRATEFUL FOR...

_____

_____

_____

_____

I GO TO BED FEELING...

_____

_____

_____

_____

TOMORROW I WISH TO...

_____

_____

_____

_____

Day 12
WALKING MEDITATIONS
Inspired by Thich Nhat Hanh (1926-2022)
Renowned Zen teacher and poet.

Feeling stressed out? Need to clear your mind? Feel Stuck? Go take a walk! Walking meditations work at helping you mentally by boosting your mood and physically by just moving the body and boosting the blood flow. For even more meditative benefits, try finding and walking a Labyrinth or get more grounded by kicking off your shoes and walking outside! Walking Meditations were really made more popular by Thich Nhat Hanh. He reminded us that we are often walking from point A to B. We become so focused on the end point that get detached from the world around that is happening all around us and rush through the steps so fast that we never appreciate the journey.

Stop looking down and texting while your walk! How about looking up? Look straight ahead. Smile and be an integral part of your own journey. When you slow down your walking, you start to step with reverence and instead of an external destination, you start to walk to that sacred place within. When you connect with your breath you connect with source. You remember that the Earth is sacred and you get to connect with her and the rest of nature and all of its gifts that are surrounding us. We begin to "stop and smell the roses." We stop from moving rotely and begin to see and appreciate the magic all around us. The every day miracles. We realize we are not lost. We are in fact coming home. Home to this present moment. There is no need to rush. You have already arrived. With each breath take one step. I have arrived. Then try to slow down even more and take several breaths for each single breath. The mind may fight you and want to stop and run but remain steadfast. This is a skill to be developed. You are teaching your body and mind the importance of slowing down, that you are safe in your own body and that there is no need to run. After a few minutes you will feel yourself quieting down. Bear witness to what is happening. To the thoughts. Ask yourself what is this moment trying to teach me? Notice your surroundings? Do you notice anything new? What are the smells? What are the sensations? What is the surface of where you are walking (wet grass, sand, hot, cool)? Where are you being lead? Pay attention to your stride and the sole of your foot. Feel the gravity pull you back to Earth. Notice if your balance is steady or not. Smile at the knowing you are home. Smile with the knowing that you are exactly where you are meant to be in this precise moment.

Try to dedicate 30 minutes. Invite a friend or walk while in your next meeting. Find ways to incorporate mindful walking in your day to day routines.
The famous quote from Gandalf in The Hobbit:
"A wizard is never late, nor is he early, he arrives precisely when he means to."

PRE-MEDITATION - MIND DUMP - 3 MINUTE JOURNALING

Daily

Morning

Meditation

_____
_____
_____
_____
_____

_____
_____
_____
_____

DURATION & TYPE OF MEDITATION

○ _____
○ _____
○ _____

WHAT INSPIRED YOU THE MOST TODAY? MANTRA USED OR REFLECTIONS

WHAT EMOTIONS HAVE YOU FELT TODAY?

OTHER EXPERIENCES & OBSERVATIONS

○ _____
○ _____
○ _____

HOW WOULD YOU RATE THE SESSIION?

☆ ☆ ☆ ☆ ☆

Evening Meditation

For your second meditation, take a few minutes to quickly recap your day from the moment you woke up to the present moment. Replay the day - interactions and decisions. Don't get stuck. Practice acknowledgement and non-attachment. Observe. Take in the lesson and make a mental note on how you would have handled differently. Let it all go in peace.

TODAY I LEARNED....

_____

_____

_____

_____

I AM GRATFUL FOR...

_____

_____

_____

_____

I GO TO BED FEELING...

_____

_____

_____

_____

TOMORROW I WISH TO...

_____

_____

_____

_____

Day 13

I AM HERE
TO BE SEEN!

I AM HERE
AND I SEE YOU!

TODAY WE ARE SPEAKING
TO OUR OWN SOULS

EXERCISE: AFFIRMATIONS TO BE SAID WHILE LOOKING IN THE MIRROR AT YOUR OWN REFLECTION- LOOK INTO YOUR EYES DEEPLY AND STATE, "SIKHONA," WHICH MEANS "I AM HERE TO BE SEEN." TAKE A FEW BREATHS AND DO NOT LOOK AWAY. THEN STATE, "SAWUBONA," WHICH MEANS "I SEE YOU." ** THIS IS ALSO THE ZULU GREETING EXPLAINED BELOW

I ask you, what do you see when you look in the mirror? Do you see perfection? You should!

Now, let's explore the history of this greeting. We all know there is power in words and this greeting is one that surely invokes the spirit. I encourage you to teach this greeting to your friends, whether it be in English or original Zulu language. I find both are just as powerful. Sikhona is what is said as you greet the person. Sawubona is the response greeting.

This greeting represents the Zulu philosophy of ubuntu, which in its simplest translation would mean "togetherness," or more profoundly, "I am because you are." It has the same energy of the "I am that I am" Biblical energy. When one person says, "I am here to be seen," that person's spirit is invoked to be fully present in the moment, signaling a willingness to engage with integrity. To be seen emphasizes the removal of masks. The exposing of our true essence, the real you at the core, no lies, label, deception or defenses. You engage on the same level with the other person. The moment you hear the response, "I see you," simply hearing this affirmation that you are seen hits you at the soul level. It is that deep "waiting to exhale" moment of acknowledgment that someone not only sees you, but sees you as God made you. Innately, you will engage in that soul contact as your eyes will magnetically seek each other in acknowledgment and reverence.

For some, that moment is magically healing because for so long all we have wanted was to be seen. You have to believe and know that you matter and are loved without judgment or conditions. This is why I offer it to you today as an exercise to greet yourself in the mirror. You deserve to be seen and respected here, now, and every moment you walk on this Earth! Do this exercise daily. Once you can see with this lens, you can see this essence in others.

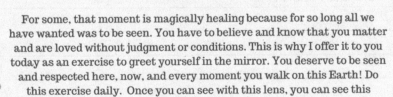

PRE-MEDITATION - MIND DUMP - 3 MINUTE JOURNALING

Daily

Morning

Meditation

DURATION & TYPE OF MEDITATION

○

○

○

WHAT INSPIRED YOU THE MOST TODAY? MANTRA USED OR REFLECTIONS

WHAT EMOTIONS HAVE YOU FELT TODAY?

OTHER EXPERIENCES & OBSERVATIONS

○

○

○

HOW WOULD YOU RATE THE SESSIION?

☆ ☆ ☆ ☆ ☆

Evening Meditation

For your second meditation, take a few minutes to quickly recap your day from the moment you woke up to the present moment. Replay the day - interactions and decisions. Don't get stuck. Practice acknowledgement and non-attachment. Observe. Take in the lesson and make a mental note on how you would have handled differently. Let it all go in peace.

TODAY I LEARNED....

_____

_____

_____

_____

I AM GRATEFUL FOR...

_____

_____

_____

_____

I GO TO BED FEELING...

_____

_____

_____

_____

TOMORROW I WISH TO...

_____

_____

_____

_____

Day 14

MANTRA: NAM MYOHO RENGE KYO

Myoho Renge Kyo was first derived in Chinese, as the title of the enlighten Lotus Sutra. It was the taught by Siddharta Gautama Buddha in India around 2,500 years ago. This mantra could be defined as a vow, an expression of determination, to embrace and manifest our true Buddha nature during times of difficulties and to achieve more bliss and less suffering.

- NAM - this syllable represents "devotion to" or "I take refuge within." Also, root of the Sanskrit term "namah," which translates as "devotion" or "commitment."
- Myoho - this syllable represents the mystic laws of Karma and cause and effect. "Mio" has also been interpreted as "the constant truth."
- Renge - this syllable symbolizes the lotus flower (a resilient flower that simultaneously blooms and seeds).
- Kyo - this syllable represents the power of sound (vibration). Kyo also signifies the sutras, the teachings of Buddha and the energy of creation and manifesting.

Lotus Hand Mudra shown above can be activated to bring in strength, loving attitude towards others, creates a relaxed mind and body.

Give yourself the credit you deserve for getting this far. You are a survivor.

No mud, No Lotus. I am resilient

I will always rise up! I always find a way!

Behind every cloud is a blue sky. After the storm is always a rainbow

I sit and find stillness. I am the calm in the storm

I am Healing, Growing, Resilient, Blessed & Shining with Divine Light!

Weekly Wellness check in

DATE _____

HOW DOES YOUR BODY FEEL
TODAY? DID YOU MOVE THIS
WEEK? HOW WAS YOUR DIET?

WHAT FELT GOOD THIS WEEK?

○ _____
○ _____
○ _____
○ _____

ARE YOU IN BALANCE?

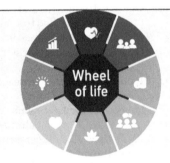

MARK IF YOU FEEL ANY PAIN

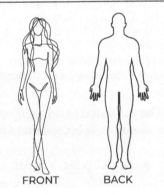

FRONT   BACK

3 AREAS I NEED TO FOCUS ON

_____
○ _____
○ _____
○ _____

WHICH EMOTIONS WERE
PREDOMINANT THIS WEEK?

MENTAL OUTLOOK - HOW
INSPIRED WERE YOU THIS WEEK?

☆ ☆ ☆ ☆ ☆

PRE-MEDITATION - MIND DUMP - 3 MINUTE JOURNALING

Daily

Morning

Meditation

_____

_____

_____

_____

_____

_____

_____

_____

_____

_____

DURATION & TYPE OF MEDITATION

○ _____

○ _____

○ _____

WHAT INSPIRED YOU THE MOST TODAY? MANTRA USED OR REFLECTIONS

WHAT EMOTIONS HAVE YOU FELT TODAY?

OTHER EXPERIENCES & OBSERVATIONS

○ _____

○ _____

○ _____

HOW WOULD YOU RATE THE SESSIION?

☆ ☆ ☆ ☆ ☆

Evening Meditation

For your second meditation, take a few minutes to quickly recap your day from the moment you woke up to the present moment. Replay the day - interactions and decisions. Don't get stuck. Practice acknowledgement and non-attachment. Observe. Take in the lesson and make a mental note on how you would have handled differently. Let it all go in peace.

TODAY I LEARNED....

_____

_____

_____

_____

I AM GRATFUL FOR...

_____

_____

_____

I GO TO BED FEELING...

_____

_____

_____

TOMORROW I WISH TO...

_____

_____

_____

Weekly Meditation check in

DATE _____

TOP 3 THINGS I DID THIS WEEK

- ○ _____
- ○ _____
- ○ _____

MOST REWARDING INTERACTION I HAD THIS WEEK

THIS WEEK I FELT

THIS WEEK I NOTICED A SHIFT IN...

_____

_____

_____

_____

NEXT WEEK I WANT TO...

WHAT WAS MY FAVORITE REFLECTION THIS WEEK?

MY RANKING OF THE WEEK

☆ ☆ ☆ ☆ ☆

TEA MEDITATION

The Japanese tea ceremony influenced the Zen Buddhism tea meditation. Overall they are all performed in the same purposeful, contemplative and mindful way. Give it a try, even if it has to be with your cup of coffee.

BOIL THE WATER

The only aim of this type of meditation is to pay attention to the tea only and nothing else. So, when you're boiling the water you should do only that. Relax and watch the bubbles go from tiny ones to big exploding ones. What are the sounds that the water makes? Let the sounds of water set the atmosphere.

This is an important step Ayurvedically speaking because the belief is that there is energy in the fire that is infused into the tea. You want that element of "agni." Avoid making your tea with water from a commercial automatic hot water machine.

MIX THE WATER WITH THE TEA, not the other way around

SLOW DOWN AND BEGIN TO BECOME AWARE OF ASPECTS & NUANCES OF THE TEA

After a few minutes, gently remove the leaves and just sit with your tea for a while. This will give a chance to tea to cool a bit and to you to enjoy the aromas and colors of the brew. Take a moment and think about the leaf itself. How long and what was the process this little leaf had to go through in order to make this cup? Think about the the person who farmed it, picked it, packaged it, and transported it all to get to this moment. Offer them a moment of gratitude.

DRINK YOUR TEA

Pick up the cup with both hands. Notice how this includes all of your senses. As you sip it slowly become aware how you are interacting by bringing an element of the outside world into your inner being. Focus on the characteristics of the cup - what color is it, shape, size, material? How does the cup feel in your hands? How does the tea look inside - clear or cloudy? Pay attention to the temperature whether it is hot or cold. What about the taste - earthy, floral, fruity or grassy? How does the tea feel in your mouth - creamy, dry, heavy or light. Direct your thoughts only to the tea with each sip. Some reflections you can direct into your cup:

I am nourished.

I ignite the healing powers of this liquid. It is providing healing to my mind, spirit and body down to my cells.

I focus only on me and my complete and whole well being in this precise moment.

It is well with my soul

You will notice that each cup will bring different nuances to the experience. After you have finished drinking your tea, don't forget to enjoy the process of cleaning after yourself. This too is a part of the ceremony which will help you remain mindful.

Weekly Focus

M

T

W

WEEKLY AFFIRMATION, REFLECTION OR FOCUS

HABITS & RITUALS

Journaled	○	○	○	○	○	○	○
Connected / Prayed	○	○	○	○	○	○	○
Visualized / Goals	○	○	○	○	○	○	○
Meditation / Breathe	○	○	○	○	○	○	○
Yoga	○	○	○	○	○	○	○
Organize Space/Life	○	○	○	○	○	○	○
Self-Care	○	○	○	○	○	○	○
Played/ was Creative	○	○	○	○	○	○	○
Cooked/Ate Healthy	○	○	○	○	○	○	○
Moved / Exercised	○	○	○	○	○	○	○
Was out in Nature	○	○	○	○	○	○	○
Met a friend/Family	○	○	○	○	○	○	○
Served Community	○	○	○	○	○	○	○
Digital Detox	○	○	○	○	○	○	○

MUST DO LIST

○ _____

○ _____

○ _____

TH

F

SAT

SUN

NOTES

_____

_____

_____

_____

_____

_____

_____

_____

_____

_____

_____

_____

PRE-MEDITATION - MIND DUMP - 3 MINUTE JOURNALING

Daily

Morning

Meditation

DURATION & TYPE OF MEDITATION

○ _____

○ _____

○ _____

WHAT INSPIRED YOU THE MOST TODAY? MANTRA USED OR REFLECTIONS

WHAT EMOTIONS HAVE YOU FELT TODAY?

OTHER EXPERIENCES & OBSERVATIONS

○ _____

○ _____

○ _____

HOW WOULD YOU RATE THE SESSIION?

☆ ☆ ☆ ☆ ☆

Evening Meditation

For your second meditation, take a few minutes to quickly recap your day from the moment you woke up to the present moment. Replay the day - interactions and decisions. Don't get stuck. Practice acknowledgement and non-attachment. Observe. Take in the lesson and make a mental note on how you would have handled differently. Let it all go in peace.

TODAY I LEARNED....

_____

_____

_____

_____

I AM GRATFUL FOR...

_____

_____

_____

_____

I GO TO BED FEELING...

_____

_____

_____

_____

TOMORROW I WISH TO...

_____

_____

_____

_____

Day 16

SO VERY
thankful

INCREDIBLY
grateful

UNBELIEVABLY
blessed

We just hit the half way point. You have truly got to feel the energetic shift happening. Today is a free day to revisit your past 2 weeks of observances. Reread some of the inspired entries and even the struggles. Observe where have you seen some growth and where are you still in need of more concentrated efforts. Do you notice any patterns or habitual distractions? Where are you being pulled? Have any of the meditation techniques really been soothing? Stick with them. Have any been challenging or even triggering? Have you been making excuses? Can you lean into it and uncover why? Can you sit in the discomfort of it as a way of healing it? (** if you are seeking professional help, it may be something to bring up to your therapist.) All of this work takes dedication, discipline and most of all honesty. You have been working so hard lately. I am so proud of you!!
Be patient. Remember, you are rewiring your thought patterns and mind. There have been many recent scientific studies being conducted that have been demonstrating how meditation does heal the body and mind physically too. The work of healing and the universe happens even when and where we don't see it. Trust that you have shifted stuff and the universe is working its way to you. You can go back and revisit one of the previous mantras that you really liked, if you wanted. If not, for today. Just sit in gratitude and repeat the above affirmations.
Drop me an email or tag in a post on how you are feeling. I would love to hear from you! May the universe truly bring you all that your heart desires! You deserve it. You got this! Let Erica support your journey! Please be sure to check out Erica's other books, event, retreats, yoga teacher trainings, courses and more!
www.ericagarciayoga.com

PRE-MEDITATION - MIND DUMP - 3 MINUTE JOURNALING

Daily

Morning

Meditation

_____

_____

_____

_____

_____

_____

_____

_____

_____

DURATION & TYPE OF MEDITATION

○ _____

○ _____

○ _____

WHAT EMOTIONS HAVE YOU FELT TODAY?

HOW WOULD YOU RATE THE SESSIION?

☆ ☆ ☆ ☆ ☆

WHAT INSPIRED YOU THE MOST TODAY? MANTRA USED OR REFLECTIONS

OTHER EXPERIENCES & OBSERVATIONS

○ _____

○ _____

○ _____

Evening Meditation

For your second meditation, take a few minutes to quickly recap your day from the moment you woke up to the present moment. Replay the day - interactions and decisions. Don't get stuck. Practice acknowledgement and non-attachment. Observe. Take in the lesson and make a mental note on how you would have handled differently. Let it all go in peace.

TODAY I LEARNED....

_____

_____

_____

I AM GRATFUL FOR...

_____

_____

_____

I GO TO BED FEELING...

_____

_____

_____

TOMORROW I WISH TO...

_____

_____

_____

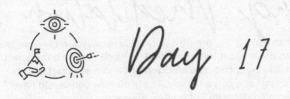 # Day 17

It is so good to ritually and continually check in and ask yourself these self reflective questions. When you sit and ask yourself and then remain in silence, the answers do come. When creating a life with purpose that is the life of your dreams there will be a lot of shifts and changes as new information and opportunities come. Above it all, you want to be able to remain true to you.

Who am I?
Why am I here?
What makes my heart happy?
What do I love? Who can I show love to?
What do I need to forgive myself for? Who can I offer forgiveness to?
What do I need? Who needs me?
Where am I thriving?
Where can I use more support?
How can I make today a better day for myself and others?
Who or what do I need to let go of in order to move forward to the life of my dreams?

AFFIRMATIONS:
I am creating the life of my dreams.
My life is in balance.
I have unlimited potential.
My commitment to myself is unbreakable.
I am living my dharma (Life Purpose).
All the visions I have in my heart and mind come to me effortlessly.
I let go of self sabotaging traits and habits. I believe in my abilities.

PRE-MEDITATION - MIND DUMP -
3 MINUTE JOURNALING

Daily

Morning

Meditation

_____

_____

_____

_____

_____

_____

_____

DURATION & TYPE OF MEDITATION

○ _____

○ _____

○ _____

WHAT INSPIRED YOU THE MOST
TODAY? MANTRA USED OR
REFLECTIONS

WHAT EMOTIONS HAVE YOU
FELT TODAY?

OTHER EXPERIENCES &
OBSERVATIONS

○ _____

HOW WOULD YOU RATE THE
SESSIION?

☆ ☆ ☆ ☆ ☆

○ _____

○ _____

Evening Meditation

For your second meditation, take a few minutes to quickly recap your day from the moment you woke up to the present moment. Replay the day - interactions and decisions. Don't get stuck. Practice acknowledgement and non-attachment. Observe. Take in the lesson and make a mental note on how you would have handled differently. Let it all go in peace.

TODAY I LEARNED....

_____

_____

_____

_____

I AM GRATFUL FOR...

_____

_____

_____

_____

I GO TO BED FEELING...

_____

_____

_____

_____

TOMORROW I WISH TO...

_____

_____

_____

_____

MANTRA : SO HUM
"I AM THAT"

The "SO HUM" mantra is also known as the Hamsa Mantra. It is one of the most important mantras in Kriya yoga and Tantrism. It can be broadly translated as "I am that", with the "that" being the essence we know as God, the great mystery, universal awareness, consciousness, source and presence. While meditating and silently repeating the mantra in our minds, the mantra has the power to bring us to the core of our being, that place where "source" or "spirit" resides. For this practice, it is advised that you repeat the mantra mentally to realize the full benefit and potential.

It is even more resonate to coordinate the breath pattern because many often also equate the "SO HUM" as the actual words of our breath (or prana, our life giving force) With your inhale breath you can repeat in your mind the word for the sound of the inhale breath, "SO, and next you would repeat the word for the sound of the exhale "HAM" as you released your breath. If you choose to just repeat the mantra in English, it would inhale "I AM," and exhale "THAT" or you can finish the "I AM" statement with whatever you wish to declare on your exhale. Continue to ride the rhythm of your breath and continue to repeat the mantra all with the awareness and intent on connecting to the true essence and magnificence of the source that is truly with you and all.

HAMSA FACTS : Hamsa comes from the Hebrew word Hamesh, the word for the number five. It is viewed as a symbol for the "Hand of God" or also known as the Hand of Miriam (sister to Moses and Aaron in Judaism) or Fatima (daughter of Prophet Mohammed in Islam). There is also a significance to the five senses that God blesses you with. What many don't realize is that when the fingers are pointed up, it signifies Gods protection from evil and can bring in more harmony shielding you from the evil inner thoughts of others such as hatred, insecurities and jealousy. When the fingers are facing downward, it is believed that the hand in this direction is to bring good Karma, Abundance and Blessings from God. Also, the guided hand to bring your good luck, answers to your prayers and manifestations to life

PRE-MEDITATION - MIND DUMP - 3 MINUTE JOURNALING

Daily

Morning

Meditation

_____

_____

_____

_____

_____

_____

_____

_____

_____

_____

DURATION & TYPE OF MEDITATION

○ _____

○ _____

○ _____

WHAT INSPIRED YOU THE MOST TODAY? MANTRA USED OR REFLECTIONS

WHAT EMOTIONS HAVE YOU FELT TODAY?

HOW WOULD YOU RATE THE SESSIION?

☆ ☆ ☆ ☆ ☆

OTHER EXPERIENCES & OBSERVATIONS

○ _____

○ _____

○ _____

Evening Meditation

For your second meditation, take a few minutes to quickly recap your day from the moment you woke up to the present moment. Replay the day - interactions and decisions. Don't get stuck. Practice acknowledgement and non-attachment. Observe. Take in the lesson and make a mental note on how you would have handled differently. Let it all go in peace.

TODAY I LEARNED....

_____

_____

_____

_____

I AM GRATFUL FOR...

_____

_____

_____

_____

I GO TO BED FEELING...

_____

_____

_____

_____

TOMORROW I WISH TO...

_____

_____

_____

_____

Day 19

MANTRA: ATHA
"NOW"

I have arrived to this present moment. I am present in this moment. I am here right now. I am open to receive. I am living in the now.

The moment is "NOW"

As a yoga teacher, I am always teaching from the place of now. The very first sutra from the Yoga Sutras of Patanjali (1.1) states, "Atha Yoga Anusasanam." This translates to Now is the moment that the teachings of Yoga will begin. It is not about touching your toes. It is about embodying the philosophical and vast teachings of yoga and when you do... the yoga, that union we seek with our bodies, minds and spirits will begin.

Atha

So, I encourage you to sit and explore the "Now." It allows you to sit in your stillness. It allows you to let go of that which is worrying you, bringing up fear. Who are you, right now? How are you, right now? What do you feel, right now? What can you let go of, right now? Can you bring your body and mind to this very precise moment, the "Now?" It can be very freeing when you can just be. Be who you are. Accept who you are right here, right now. Just breath. You need to do nothing more or nothing less. Just bear witness to all the gifts and blessings you possess in this moment. Remain grateful. Remain present.

Repeat in your minds voice calmly... atha, atha, atha

PRE-MEDITATION - MIND DUMP - 3 MINUTE JOURNALING

Daily

Morning

Meditation

_____
_____
_____
_____
_____
_____

_____
_____
_____
_____
_____

DURATION & TYPE OF MEDITATION

○ _____

○ _____

○ _____

WHAT INSPIRED YOU THE MOST TODAY? MANTRA USED OR REFLECTIONS

WHAT EMOTIONS HAVE YOU FELT TODAY?

OTHER EXPERIENCES & OBSERVATIONS

○ _____

○ _____

○ _____

HOW WOULD YOU RATE THE SESSIION?

☆ ☆ ☆ ☆ ☆

Evening Meditation

For your second meditation, take a few minutes to quickly recap your day from the moment you woke up to the present moment. Replay the day - interactions and decisions. Don't get stuck. Practice acknowledgement and non-attachment. Observe. Take in the lesson and make a mental note on how you would have handled differently. Let it all go in peace.

TODAY I LEARNED....

_____

_____

_____

I AM GRATFUL FOR...

_____

_____

_____

I GO TO BED FEELING...

_____

_____

_____

TOMORROW I WISH TO...

_____

_____

_____

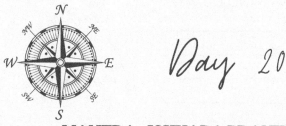

MANTRA : ISHVARA PRANIDHANA

"God, what will you have me do? Whatever is thy
Will, It is my Will to do it. Guide my steps
towards you and my True Purpose (North) here
on Earth."

ISHVARA is a Sanskrit word that can be translated as
"supreme, God, the Absolute Brahman, True Self, or one's
unchanging Reality."
PRANIDHANA has been translated as "dedication, devotion, or
surrender."

Therefore, this mantra can be a true surrender to the Diving to
help guide you and pull your inner compass towards YOUR
TRUE NORTH. When in search for the meaning of life, the
comprehension of your essence of being? Do you seek to
understand the nature of your Soul and your true purpose?
When you practice Ishvara Pranidhana, one dedicates their
merits to the Divine and yourself to what you are truly here to
do and what you truly love, as well as, serving the greater
good. When a person practices Ishvara Pranidhana, they
dedicate the merits of their actions and every step they take
(all actions, thoughts, words) with walking along side with the
Divine. The focus is less on looking for personal gain, and their
actions are more guided by humility, sincerity and serving yes,
themselves but more for the greater good. They know that the
rest will be provided.

PRE-MEDITATION - MIND DUMP - 3 MINUTE JOURNALING

Daily

Morning

Meditation

_____

_____

_____

_____

_____

_____

_____

_____

_____

_____

DURATION & TYPE OF MEDITATION

○ _____

○ _____

○ _____

WHAT EMOTIONS HAVE YOU FELT TODAY?

HOW WOULD YOU RATE THE SESSIION?

☆ ☆ ☆ ☆ ☆

WHAT INSPIRED YOU THE MOST TODAY? MANTRA USED OR REFLECTIONS

OTHER EXPERIENCES & OBSERVATIONS

○ _____

○ _____

○ _____

Evening Meditation

For your second meditation, take a few minutes to quickly recap your day from the moment you woke up to the present moment. Replay the day - interactions and decisions. Don't get stuck. Practice acknowledgement and non-attachment. Observe. Take in the lesson and make a mental note on how you would have handled differently. Let it all go in peace.

TODAY I LEARNED....

_____

_____

_____

_____

I AM GRATFUL FOR...

_____

_____

_____

_____

I GO TO BED FEELING...

_____

_____

_____

_____

TOMORROW I WISH TO...

_____

_____

_____

_____

Day 21

MANTRA: HO'OPONOPONO
The ancient Hawaiian practice of reconciliation and forgiveness.

I am Sorry.
Forgive me.
I love you.
Thank you.

Weekly Wellness check in

DATE

HOW DOES YOUR BODY FEEL
TODAY? DID YOU MOVE THIS
WEEK? HOW WAS YOUR DIET?

WHAT FELT GOOD THIS WEEK?

○
○
○
○

ARE YOU IN BALANCE?

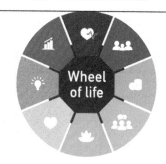

MARK IF YOU FEEL ANY PAIN

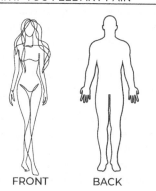

FRONT   BACK

WHICH EMOTIONS WERE PREDOMINANT THIS WEEK?

3 AREAS I NEED TO FOCUS ON

○
○
○

MENTAL OUTLOOK - HOW INSPIRED WERE YOU THIS WEEK?

PRE-MEDITATION - MIND DUMP - 3 MINUTE JOURNALING

Daily

Morning

Meditation

_____
_____
_____
_____
_____
_____
_____
_____
_____
_____

DURATION & TYPE OF MEDITATION
○ _____
○ _____
○ _____

WHAT EMOTIONS HAVE YOU FELT TODAY?

HOW WOULD YOU RATE THE SESSIION?

☆ ☆ ☆ ☆ ☆

WHAT INSPIRED YOU THE MOST TODAY? MANTRA USED OR REFLECTIONS

OTHER EXPERIENCES & OBSERVATIONS
○ _____
○ _____
○ _____

Evening Meditation

For your second meditation, take a few minutes to quickly recap your day from the moment you woke up to the present moment. Replay the day - interactions and decisions. Don't get stuck. Practice acknowledgement and non-attachment. Observe. Take in the lesson and make a mental note on how you would have handled differently. Let it all go in peace.

TODAY I LEARNED....

_____

_____

_____

_____

I AM GRATFUL FOR...

_____

_____

_____

_____

I GO TO BED FEELING...

_____

_____

_____

_____

TOMORROW I WISH TO...

_____

_____

_____

_____

Weekly Meditation check in

DATE _____

TOP 3 THINGS I DID THIS WEEK

- ○ _____
- ○ _____
- ○ _____

MOST REWARDING INTERACTION I HAD THIS WEEK

THIS WEEK I FELT

THIS WEEK I NOTICED A SHIFT IN...

_____
_____
_____
_____

NEXT WEEK I WANT TO...

WHAT WAS MY FAVORITE REFLECTION THIS WEEK?

MY RANKING OF THE WEEK

☆ ☆ ☆ ☆ ☆

MUST ORDER NEXT 30 DAY JOURNAL!!

Day 22

FULL CHAKRA BALANACING MANTRAS FROM ROOT (RED) TO CROWN (TOP OF HEAD)

LAM-VAM-RAM-YAM-HAM-OM-(silence)
UHH- OOO-OHH-AHH- EYE- AYE- EEE- (silence)

The first set are the seed sounds. The second set are the vowel sounds. Try to sit comfortably. Take a deep inhale breath and let out a big open mouth exhale. You will be chanting these out loud so that you can really bring in the energy and vibration to activate each of the seven chakras. When you repeat each sound, you can either keep your hands in Gyan mudra on your knees as in the example or you may cup your two hands and move them from point point in order to get that sound and physical body awareness. In both hand variations, be sure to envision the colors of the chakra activating. We generally start from the bottom RED. Root Chakra and work our way up when balancing and opening. When manifesting, you want to open and then work the way down to pull from the Heavens to manifest here on Earth.

I would then start back up again and repeat both lines until you have done 7 repetitions.

The left picture shows the visuals of how when you activate the "Kundalini" (serpent energy) and bring it up through the lower 5 chakras. You should envision the energy moving and crossing the body from both the left (Ida) and right (Pingala) hemispheres of the body crossing at the Chakras (across the Sushumna nadi - center line) all the way up until you have come to the 6th Chakra (center between the eyebrows). Per the ancient guidance, once the energy has centered at the 6th Chakra, your effort should then be to pull up to the Crown (7th Chakra) and out up into direct connection with source. Give it a try!

Weekly Focus

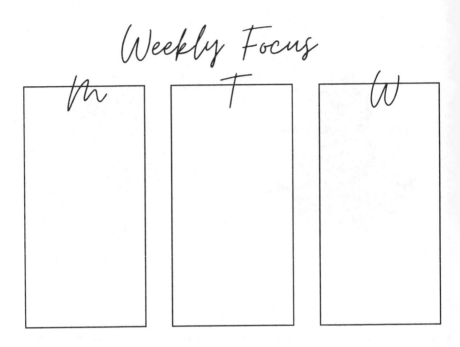

M

T

W

WEEKLY AFFIRMATION, REFLECTION OR FOCUS

HABITS & RITUALS

Journaled	○	○	○	○	○	○ ○
Connected / Prayed	○	○	○	○	○	○ ○
Visualized / Goals	○	○	○	○	○	○ ○
Meditation / Breathe	○	○	○	○	○	○ ○
Yoga	○	○	○	○	○	○ ○
Organize Space/Life	○	○	○	○	○	○ ○
Self-Care	○	○	○	○	○	○ ○
Played/ was Creative	○	○	○	○	○	○ ○
Cooked/Ate Healthy	○	○	○	○	○	○ ○
Moved / Exercised	○	○	○	○	○	○ ○
Was out in Nature	○	○	○	○	○	○ ○
Met a friend/Family	○	○	○	○	○	○ ○
Served Community	○	○	○	○	○	○ ○
Digital Detox	○	○	○	○	○	○ ○

MUST DO LIST

○ _____

○ _____

○ _____

MUST ORDER MY NEXT 30 DAY JOURNAL
CONSIDER GIFTING ONE TO A FRIEND, too!
www.ericagarciayoga.com

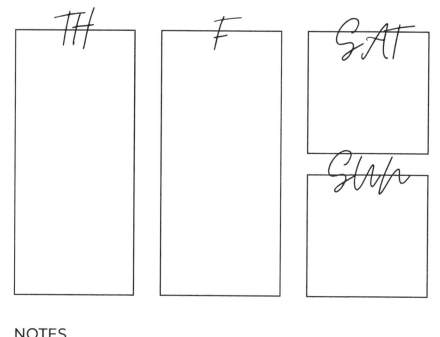

TH

F

SAT

SUN

NOTES

PRE-MEDITATION - MIND DUMP - 3 MINUTE JOURNALING

Daily

Morning

Meditation

_____

_____

_____

_____

_____

_____

_____

_____

_____

DURATION & TYPE OF MEDITATION

○ _____

○ _____

○ _____

WHAT EMOTIONS HAVE YOU FELT TODAY?

HOW WOULD YOU RATE THE SESSIION?

☆ ☆ ☆ ☆ ☆

WHAT INSPIRED YOU THE MOST TODAY? MANTRA USED OR REFLECTIONS

OTHER EXPERIENCES & OBSERVATIONS

○ _____

○ _____

○ _____

Evening Meditation

For your second meditation, take a few minutes to quickly recap your day from the moment you woke up to the present moment. Replay the day - interactions and decisions. Don't get stuck. Practice acknowledgement and non-attachment. Observe. Take in the lesson and make a mental note on how you would have handled differently. Let it all go in peace.

TODAY I LEARNED....

_____

_____

_____

_____

I AM GRATFUL FOR...

_____

_____

_____

_____

I GO TO BED FEELING...

_____

_____

_____

_____

TOMORROW I WISH TO...

_____

_____

_____

_____

Day 23

MANTRA: OM SHANTI
"I AM PEACE"

In this way, the "Om" is representing "I or myself" and "Shanti" in this mantra refers to "Peace or Silence."

Generally, the mantra is also chanted or sung as, "OM SHANTI, SHANTI, SHANTI, OM"

This mantra is pretty commonly used today but as simple as it is, it is really powerful. Let this mantra be very calming as you continue to repeat it silently to yourself.

Today may be a good day to visit a place that brings you peace. Maybe go to a park, botanical garden, church, temple, wellness retreat. Maybe spend the day in self care of mind, body and spirt. Bring your journal with you and really make a day of it.

PRE-MEDITATION - MIND DUMP - 3 MINUTE JOURNALING

Daily

Morning

Meditation

_____
_____
_____
_____
_____

_____
_____
_____
_____

DURATION & TYPE OF MEDITATION

○ _____

○ _____

○ _____

WHAT INSPIRED YOU THE MOST TODAY? MANTRA USED OR REFLECTIONS

WHAT EMOTIONS HAVE YOU FELT TODAY?

OTHER EXPERIENCES & OBSERVATIONS

○ _____

HOW WOULD YOU RATE THE SESSIION?

○ _____

☆ ☆ ☆ ☆ ☆

○ _____

Evening Meditation

For your second meditation, take a few minutes to quickly recap your day from the moment you woke up to the present moment. Replay the day - interactions and decisions. Don't get stuck. Practice acknowledgement and non-attachment. Observe. Take in the lesson and make a mental note on how you would have handled differently. Let it all go in peace.

TODAY I LEARNED....

_____

_____

_____

_____

I AM GRATFUL FOR...

_____

_____

_____

I GO TO BED FEELING...

_____

_____

_____

TOMORROW I WISH TO...

_____

_____

_____

Day 24

MANTRA: HINANI
"HEE-NAY-NEE"

HEBREW: "HERE I AM" OR "I AM HERE" AS IN AN
INNER SUBMISSIVE OFFERING TO GOD THAT YOU
ARE HERE AS IN "I AM HERE AT YOUR SERVICE" OR
"WHATEVER THY WILL, IT IS MY WILL TO DO IT."

" I lift up my eyes to the mountains—where does
my help come from? My help comes from the Lord,
the Maker of heaven and earth." (Psalm 121:1-2).

Did you ever just want to speak directly to source? It is taught
that during the event and story of when Moses encounters the
burning bush on Mt. Sinai, when the voice of God called out to
Moses, his response is, "Hinani." This is translated as "Here I
am", or "I am here." The significant word is a humble beholding,
and offering up of oneself in complete submission and service to
the great "I AM." Hinani -"I am at your service",

So, I ask you. What worries do you have in your heart? The
mountain may seem insurmountable but there is no miracle
that God cannot grant. Lift your head up in humility. Trust God
is listening. Trust help is coming. It may not be coming in the
format you expect but keep your mind and heart open. It is sure
to come. Trust and believe.

PRE-MEDITATION - MIND DUMP -
3 MINUTE JOURNALING

Daily

Morning

Meditation

_____
_____
_____
_____
_____

_____
_____
_____
_____
_____

DURATION & TYPE OF MEDITATION

○ _____
○ _____
○ _____

WHAT INSPIRED YOU THE MOST
TODAY? MANTRA USED OR
REFLECTIONS

WHAT EMOTIONS HAVE YOU
FELT TODAY?

HOW WOULD YOU RATE THE
SESSIION?

☆ ☆ ☆ ☆ ☆

OTHER EXPERIENCES &
OBSERVATIONS

○ _____
○ _____
○ _____

Evening Meditation

For your second meditation, take a few minutes to quickly recap your day from the moment you woke up to the present moment. Replay the day - interactions and decisions. Don't get stuck. Practice acknowledgement and non-attachment. Observe. Take in the lesson and make a mental note on how you would have handled differently. Let it all go in peace.

TODAY I LEARNED....

_____
_____
_____
_____

I AM GRATFUL FOR...

_____
_____
_____
_____

I GO TO BED FEELING...

_____
_____
_____
_____

TOMORROW I WISH TO...

_____
_____
_____
_____

Day 25

AFFIRMATIONS:

ALL THINGS IN LIFE MUST CHANGE. I EMBRACE CHANGE. CHANGE IS NOT ALWAYS A LOSS. I CAN ACCEPT THE CHANGES THAT ARE HAPPENING. I WILL LET GO AND LET GOD. NOTHING AND NO ONE IS FIXED AND PERMANENT. I WILL LOSEN THE GRIP THAT IS CAUSING ME TO SUFFER.

The teachings of Buddha teach us that we are all connected and the natural life cycle of all things. The Buddha teaches of the principle of Impermanence.

ALL THINGS IN LIFE ARE IMPERMANENT

Everything in this world is of the nature to be born, live, die and be born again. When you look at all things in their life cycle, you will resist gripping on to that which is of the nature to change and die. You will also not look at death as an ending but more of an opportunity to view this change as a new beginning. When you take on this mind shift, it will lead you to less suffering.

Further thoughts to help you with this concept, is that we all cling onto things and chase after that illusive desire for stability. Taking on the mindset of accepting that all things in life are of the nature to die will allow you to not get so rocked when in your mind things are out of your control. It will allow you to take a pause and take it as an invitation to contemplate your dependence and the impermanence of all things—our things, our feelings, nature, our bodies, our thoughts, our problems, our independence or dependence, our victories and failures, our very lives. This significant truth of the cycles and seasons of all things is a hard one to accept but once embodied is truly freeing. When you find yourself frustrated and suffering, ask yourself where you are gripping? What change are you resisting? What is the fear? It is OK to fear the unknown. What are you truly holding onto and is it something real or perceived? What is the current state of what you are holding onto or are you holding onto a memory of what was in hopes of getting what you had back? Take a deep breath. Allow yourself to live in the moment, accept what is. Lean into these reflections when feelings of suffering are coming up for you. It will help you get past the moment.

PRE-MEDITATION - MIND DUMP - 3 MINUTE JOURNALING

Daily

Morning

Meditation

_____

_____

_____

_____

_____

_____

_____

_____

_____

_____

DURATION & TYPE OF MEDITATION

○ _____

○ _____

○ _____

WHAT INSPIRED YOU THE MOST TODAY? MANTRA USED OR REFLECTIONS

WHAT EMOTIONS HAVE YOU FELT TODAY?

OTHER EXPERIENCES & OBSERVATIONS

○ _____

○ _____

○ _____

HOW WOULD YOU RATE THE SESSIION?

☆ ☆ ☆ ☆ ☆

Evening Meditation

For your second meditation, take a few minutes to quickly recap your day from the moment you woke up to the present moment. Replay the day - interactions and decisions. Don't get stuck. Practice acknowledgement and non-attachment. Observe. Take in the lesson and make a mental note on how you would have handled differently. Let it all go in peace.

TODAY I LEARNED....

_____

_____

_____

_____

I AM GRATFUL FOR...

_____

_____

_____

_____

I GO TO BED FEELING...

_____

_____

_____

_____

TOMORROW I WISH TO...

_____

_____

_____

_____

Day 26

bloom
WHERE YOU ARE
planted

AFFIRMATION:

I AM DEEPLY ROOTED. I LET GO OF THE PAST AND WILL GROW FROM RIGHT HERE, RIGHT NOW. I AM BLOOMING WHERE GOD HAS PLANTED ME. ALLTHAT I PUTTING MY ENERGY TO IS BEARING RICH FRUIT.

Sometimes we get to stuck in the disappointment of not achieving what we envisioned that we don't see the opportunity that is staring us right in the face. God has blessed you with certain abilities that only you can offer. That is why this meditation journal has been so crucial at you reaching the dreams you have in your heart. If you continue to dedicate the time and share your God-given talents, you glorify Him and bless others. Revisit (water) your vision boards and goals. You may realize you are closer to achieving them as you thought or maybe taking on this new mindset will pivot you in a different direction. Meditate on what is in your heart today and bloom from where you are planted.

Today is inspired by the following scriptures:

- Saint Francis de Sales (1567-1622), this Bishop was recorded as saying: "Truly charity has no limit; for the love of God has been poured into our hearts by His Spirit dwelling in each one of us, calling us to a life of devotion and inviting us to bloom in the garden where He has planted and directing us to radiate the beauty and spread the fragrance of His Providence."

- God has planted you where you are that you might be a blessing. He wants you to take deep root. He wants you to bear rich fruit. And if you will draw upon His spiritual power, He will enable you to be a blessing. Bloom where you are planted and bear fruit to the glory of God and the enrichment of others.
  ~Psalm 80:8-13

PRE-MEDITATION - MIND DUMP -
3 MINUTE JOURNALING

Daily

Morning

Meditation

_____

_____

_____

_____

_____

_____

_____

_____

_____

DURATION & TYPE OF MEDITATION

○ _____

○ _____

○ _____

WHAT EMOTIONS HAVE YOU FELT TODAY?

HOW WOULD YOU RATE THE SESSIION?

☆ ☆ ☆ ☆ ☆

WHAT INSPIRED YOU THE MOST TODAY? MANTRA USED OR REFLECTIONS

OTHER EXPERIENCES & OBSERVATIONS

○ _____

○ _____

○ _____

Evening Meditation

For your second meditation, take a few minutes to quickly recap your day from the moment you woke up to the present moment. Replay the day - interactions and decisions. Don't get stuck. Practice acknowledgement and non-attachment. Observe. Take in the lesson and make a mental note on how you would have handled differently. Let it all go in peace.

TODAY I LEARNED....

_____

_____

_____

_____

I AM GRATFUL FOR...

_____

_____

_____

_____

I GO TO BED FEELING...

_____

_____

_____

_____

TOMORROW I WISH TO...

_____

_____

_____

_____

AFFIRMATIONS

Optimal Health is my natural state of being.

I am healed. I am healing.

My body is my temple. I treat it with respect and reverence.

Every Cell in my body is alive. I listen to my body and give it what it needs.

I feel healthy and full of energy.

I choose to be healthy.

I am free from pain.

I am blessed with good health.

I am being healed and restored in places I didn't even know I needed healing.

PRE-MEDITATION - MIND DUMP - 3 MINUTE JOURNALING

Daily

Morning

Meditation

_____

_____

_____

_____

_____

_____

_____

_____

DURATION & TYPE OF MEDITATION

○ _____

○ _____

○ _____

WHAT INSPIRED YOU THE MOST TODAY? MANTRA USED OR REFLECTIONS

WHAT EMOTIONS HAVE YOU FELT TODAY?

OTHER EXPERIENCES & OBSERVATIONS

○ _____

○ _____

○ _____

HOW WOULD YOU RATE THE SESSIION?

☆ ☆ ☆ ☆ ☆

Evening Meditation

For your second meditation, take a few minutes to quickly recap your day from the moment you woke up to the present moment. Replay the day - interactions and decisions. Don't get stuck. Practice acknowledgement and non-attachment. Observe. Take in the lesson and make a mental note on how you would have handled differently. Let it all go in peace.

TODAY I LEARNED....

_____
_____
_____
_____

I AM GRATFUL FOR...

_____
_____
_____

I GO TO BED FEELING...

_____
_____
_____

TOMORROW I WISH TO...

_____
_____
_____

Blessed Day 28

We will spend the next two days with the two mantras below to align you with the universal flow and energize manifesting. I provide you with a list of affirmations to help inspire your thoughts in the area you wish to focus your energy on. These practices of writing out affirmations, as well as, speaking them can be helpful in propelling you forward on your path of personal transformation.

MANTRAS FOR ALIGNING WITH THE UNIVERSE:

AHAM BRAHMASMI

Stemming from the Upanishads, it translates as "I am Brahma(God)" but used more as in the deep knowing that at the core of your being is the ultimate reality, the root and ground of the universe, the source of all that exists. That you have God within and are flowing with that God/Source energy.

SAT, CHIT, ANANDA

Sat (Existence/absolute Truth), Chit (Consciousness), Ananda (Bliss) These are three root Sanskrit words that when put together bring the vibration and energy of "Pure Bliss Consciousness"

369 MANIFESTING

Most consider the 369 manifesting techniques the best way to manifest. There are two ways to do it. Use the one that resonates with you. You can also use the pages in the back of the book to help you.

1. Write down a chosen affirmation 3 times in the morning, 6 times in the afternoon, and 9 times at night.
2. Pick 3 affirmations, repeating them 6 times a day, and focusing on your wants for 9 seconds.

Weekly Wellness check in

DATE

HOW DOES YOUR BODY FEEL
TODAY? DID YOU MOVE THIS
WEEK? HOW WAS YOUR DIET?

WHAT FELT GOOD THIS WEEK?

○ _____
○ _____
○ _____
○ _____

ARE YOU IN BALANCE?

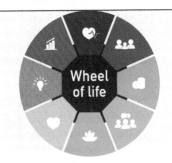

MARK IF YOU FEEL ANY PAIN

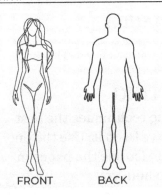

FRONT   BACK

3 AREAS I NEED TO FOCUS ON

○ _____
○ _____
○ _____

WHICH EMOTIONS WERE
PREDOMINANT THIS WEEK?

MENTAL OUTLOOK - HOW
INSPIRED WERE YOU THIS WEEK?

PRE-MEDITATION - MIND DUMP - 3 MINUTE JOURNALING

Daily

Morning

Meditation

_____

_____

_____

_____

_____

_____

_____

_____

_____

_____

DURATION & TYPE OF MEDITATION

○ _____

○ _____

○ _____

WHAT INSPIRED YOU THE MOST TODAY? MANTRA USED OR REFLECTIONS

WHAT EMOTIONS HAVE YOU FELT TODAY?

HOW WOULD YOU RATE THE SESSIION?

☆ ☆ ☆ ☆ ☆

OTHER EXPERIENCES & OBSERVATIONS

○ _____

○ _____

○ _____

Evening Meditation

For your second meditation, take a few minutes to quickly recap your day from the moment you woke up to the present moment. Replay the day - interactions and decisions. Don't get stuck. Practice acknowledgement and non-attachment. Observe. Take in the lesson and make a mental note on how you would have handled differently. Let it all go in peace.

TODAY I LEARNED....

_____

_____

_____

_____

I AM GRATFUL FOR...

_____

_____

_____

_____

I GO TO BED FEELING...

_____

_____

_____

_____

TOMORROW I WISH TO...

_____

_____

_____

_____

Weekly Meditation check in

DATE _____

TOP 3 THINGS I DID THIS WEEK
- _____
- _____
- _____

MOST REWARDING INTERACTION I HAD THIS WEEK

THIS WEEK I FELT

THIS WEEK I NOTICED A SHIFT IN...

_____

_____

_____

_____

NEXT WEEK I WANT TO...

WHAT WAS MY FAVORITE REFLECTION THIS WEEK?

MY RANKING OF THE WEEK
☆ ☆ ☆ ☆ ☆

Keep the momentum going!
Prepare for your next 30 day journal!

Day 29

I am blessed. I am favored. I AM THRIVING!
I am living in a state of abundance!
I have everything I need to be successful!
I am my best source of motivation!
I attract miracles in my life!
I am open to receiving unexpected opportunities!
I am capable of achieving greatness!
I am grateful for the abundance that I have and the abundance that's on its way!
I attract money to me easily and effortlessly!
I am worthy of the wealth/relationship/home/career I desire!
I am financially free!
I am aligned with the energy of abundance in ____!
I am capable of overcoming any money obstacles and fears that are standing in my way!
I am open to creative possibilities to get _____!
I accept and receive unexpected money!
I attract loving and positive people into my life!
I am proud of the person I am and the person I'm becoming!
I am aligned with the energy of _____!
Every moment of every day, I live my life abundantly.
I am letting go of the_____ so that the universe can bring me _____ effortlessly!
I expect and accept abundance to flow easily to me and through me!
I am Limitless in my Potential, I can create anything, anytime, anywhere!
I use my conscious intention to manifest my dreams!
I invite unlimited abundance into my life!
Today, I will focus on what I want to attract into my life.
I am calling forth the energy of God and the universe to bring me _____ or better!
I am God in Action!
I am stepping into my greatness!
I am a source of inspiration, love, and happiness!
I am healthy. My body is rejuvenating and healing as I command it!

Weekly Focus

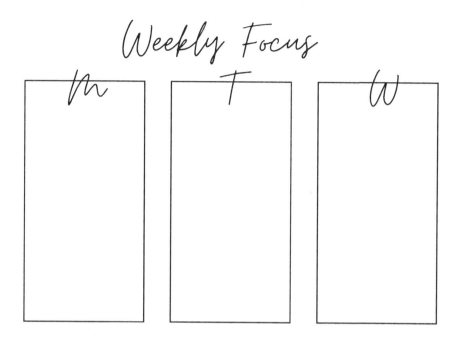

M

T

W

WEEKLY AFFIRMATION, REFLECTION OR FOCUS

HABITS & RITUALS

Journaled	○	○	○	○	○	○
Connected / Prayed	○	○	○	○	○	○
Visualized / Goals	○	○	○	○	○	○
Meditation / Breathe	○	○	○	○	○	○
Yoga	○	○	○	○	○	○
Organize Space/Life	○	○	○	○	○	○
Self-Care	○	○	○	○	○	○
Played/ was Creative	○	○	○	○	○	○
Cooked/Ate Healthy	○	○	○	○	○	○
Moved / Exercised	○	○	○	○	○	○
Was out in Nature	○	○	○	○	○	○
Met a friend/Family	○	○	○	○	○	○
Served Community	○	○	○	○	○	○
Digital Detox	○	○	○	○	○	○

MUST DO LIST

○ _____

○ _____

○ _____

MOVE GOAL TO NEW 30 DAY JOURNAL

TH

F

SAT

SUN

NOTES
_____
_____
_____
_____
_____
_____
_____
_____
_____
_____
_____
_____
_____
_____

PRE-MEDITATION - MIND DUMP - 3 MINUTE JOURNALING

Daily

Morning

Meditation

_____

_____

_____

_____

_____

_____

_____

_____

_____

_____

DURATION & TYPE OF MEDITATION

○ _____

○ _____

○ _____

WHAT INSPIRED YOU THE MOST TODAY? MANTRA USED OR REFLECTIONS

WHAT EMOTIONS HAVE YOU FELT TODAY?

OTHER EXPERIENCES & OBSERVATIONS

○ _____

○ _____

○ _____

HOW WOULD YOU RATE THE SESSIION?

☆ ☆ ☆ ☆ ☆

Evening Meditation

For your second meditation, take a few minutes to quickly recap your day from the moment you woke up to the present moment. Replay the day - interactions and decisions. Don't get stuck. Practice acknowledgement and non-attachment. Observe. Take in the lesson and make a mental note on how you would have handled differently. Let it all go in peace.

TODAY I LEARNED....

_____

_____

_____

_____

I AM GRATFUL FOR...

_____

_____

_____

I GO TO BED FEELING...

_____

_____

_____

TOMORROW I WISH TO...

_____

_____

_____

Faith Day 30 Patience

PRAYER AS MANTRA: PEACE PRAYER : English translation:

Lord, make me an instrument of your peace.
Where there is hatred, let me bring love.
Where there is offence, let me bring pardon.
Where there is discord, let me bring union.
Where there is error, let me bring truth.
Where there is doubt, let me bring faith.
Where there is despair, let me bring hope.
Where there is darkness, let me bring your light.
Where there is sadness, let me bring joy.
O Master, let me not seek as much
to be consoled as to console,
to be understood as to understand,
to be loved as to love,
for it is in giving that one receives,
it is in self-forgetting that one finds,
it is in pardoning that one is pardoned,
it is in dying that one is raised to eternal life.

I am sorry to break it to you but the prayer more popularly known as, "The prayer of St. Francis," was not written by him. Its first known occurrence was in French, in a magazine called La Clochette, published by a Catholic organization in Paris named La Ligue de la Sainte-Messe. The author's name was not given. The prayer was circulating in the USA by Jan. 1927, when its first known English version (slightly abridged from the 1912 French original) appeared in the Quaker magazine Friends' Intelligencer, under the misattributed and misspelled title "A prayer of St. Francis of Assissi."In most of the published versions of the prayer remains abridged, paraphrased or copyrighted. Above is the English translation of the complete original text from its earliest known publication (1912, copyright expired).

Finally, embrace surrender and having the Faith of a Farmer. The past 30 days have been a deep journey. You have planted many seeds. God has taught us that we have the world in the palms of our hands. Be patient. Continue respect the laws of nature. Tend to your soil. Weed it. Farmers weather the storms and remain in the state of faith and patience because they know the harvest season will come.

Genesis 1:29 God said, 'Behold, I have given you every plant yielding seed that is on the face of all the earth, and every tree with seed in its fruit. You shall have them for food.'" Ecclesiastes has this further advice, found in 11:4: "Farmers who wait for perfect weather never plant. If they watch every cloud, they never harvest," and in 11:6, "Plant your seed in the morning and keep busy all afternoon, for you don't know if profit will come from one activity or the another — or maybe both."

PRE-MEDITATION - MIND DUMP - 3 MINUTE JOURNALING

Daily

Morning

Meditation

_____
_____
_____
_____
_____
_____

_____
_____
_____
_____

DURATION & TYPE OF MEDITATION

○ _____

○ _____

○ _____

WHAT INSPIRED YOU THE MOST TODAY? MANTRA USED OR REFLECTIONS

WHAT EMOTIONS HAVE YOU FELT TODAY?

OTHER EXPERIENCES & OBSERVATIONS

HOW WOULD YOU RATE THE SESSIION?

○ _____

○ _____

○ _____

☆ ☆ ☆ ☆ ☆

Evening Meditation

For your second meditation, take a few minutes to quickly recap your day from the moment you woke up to the present moment. Replay the day - interactions and decisions. Don't get stuck. Practice acknowledgement and non-attachment. Observe. Take in the lesson and make a mental note on how you would have handled differently. Let it all go in peace.

TODAY I LEARNED....

_____

_____

_____

I AM GRATFUL FOR...

_____

_____

_____

I GO TO BED FEELING...

_____

_____

_____

TOMORROW I WISH TO...

_____

_____

_____

Final Meditation check in

DATE _____

TOP 3 THINGS I LEARNED ABOUT MYSELF IN THE PAST 30 DAYS

○ _____

○ _____

○ _____

MOST REWARDING INTERACTION I HAD DURING THIS JOURNEY

_____

OVERALL THIS PAST MONTH I FELT

THE BIGGEST SHIFT I NOTICED WAS...

_____

_____

_____

_____

NEXT 30 DAYS I WANT TO...

WHAT WAS THE LONGEST TIME I WAS ABLE TO SIT IN MEDITATION?

MY RANKING OF THE 30 DAY JOURNEY

☆ ☆ ☆ ☆ ☆

Your feedback is important! Please provide me with a review or email me your comments and a testimonial to erica@ericagarciayoga.com

Final Wellness check in

DATE _____

DID YOU NOTICE ANY NEW SELF
AWARENESSES IN YOUR BODY
THIS PAST MONTH?
_____

HOW DID YOU KEEP UP WITH
SELF-CARE THIS MONTH?

○ _____

○ _____

○ _____

○ _____

DO YOU FIND MORE BALANCE?

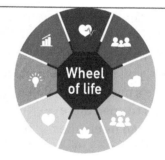

MARK IF YOU FEEL ANY PAIN

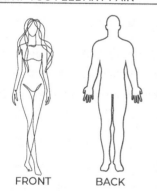

FRONT   BACK

3 AREAS I NEED TO FOCUS ON
NEXT MONTH

○ _____

○ _____

○ _____

WHICH EMOTIONS WERE
PREDOMINANT THIS MONTH?

MENTAL OUTLOOK - HOW
INSPIRED WERE YOU? DID YOUR
MENTAL OUTLOOK IMPROVE?

Final Thoughts

Wow! You did it!! This month's journey was so powerful... Don't lose the momentum! Tomorrow, start at day 1 again! If not, make the commitment to do it again in three or six months!!

I hope you felt the love I put into this journal. I thank you for allowing me to be the catalyst to help you clarifying the steps to put you in alignment of what it is you wish to achieve and your life's purpose. We don't find out life's purpose, we can actually need to open our eyes and heart, peeling away the layers of what has had us clouded to rediscover it. Remember, the answers and the power is always with and in you. You just have to trust it. My wish is that you truly put your heart into it. You get what you put your energy to. I pray that you truly have healed and opened yourself to writing into existence all the dreams you desire.

The universe is always listening.

Keep the faith!!

Please provide me with a review and testimonials!
please consider gifting this book to your friends and family!
Please consider gathering as a group and do it together as a 30 day book club.
Please join my community! Join my daily morning meditations!

God's Whispers.

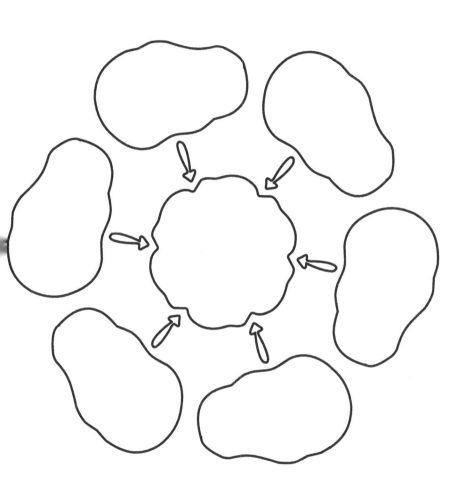

God's Whispers.

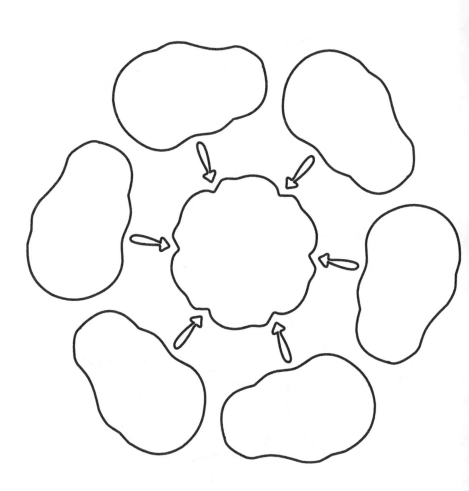

God's Whispers.

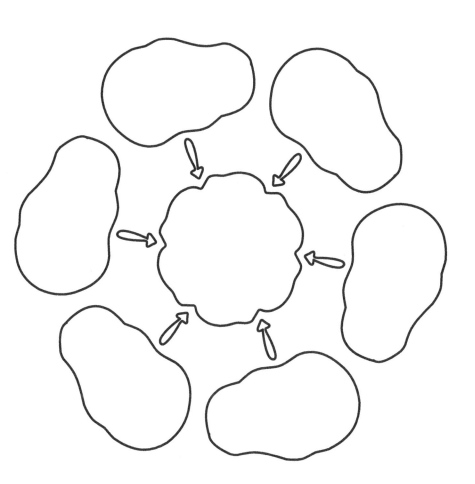

God's Whispers.

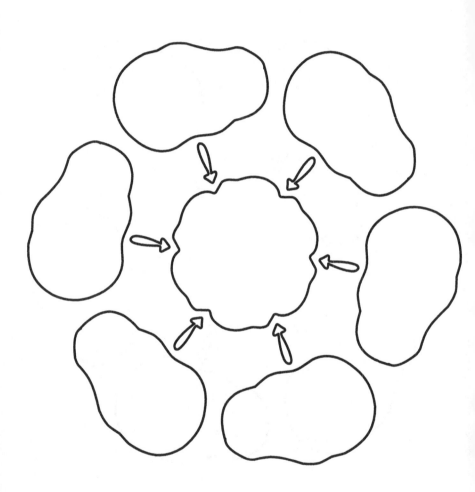

God's Whispers.

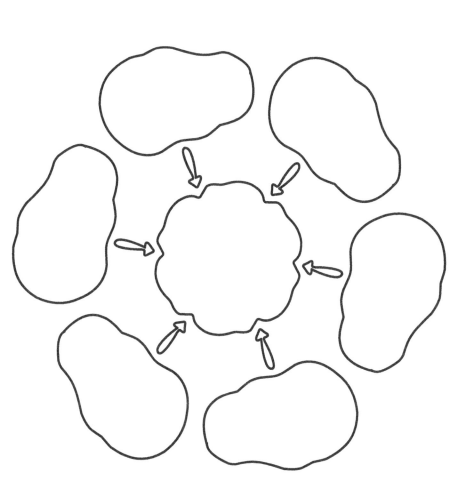

Sacred Geomrty

Dristi Meditation

Breath & Focus on the center dot

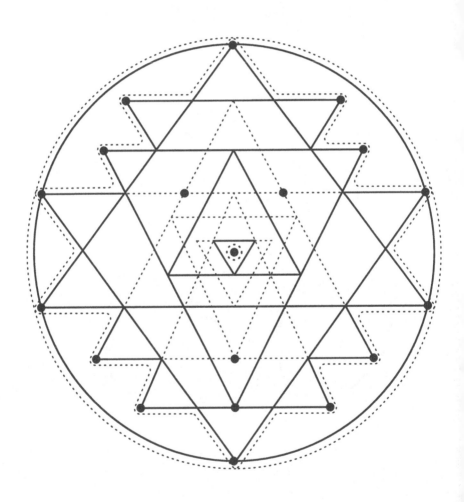

Sacred Geomrty

Dristi Meditation

Breath & Focus on the center dot

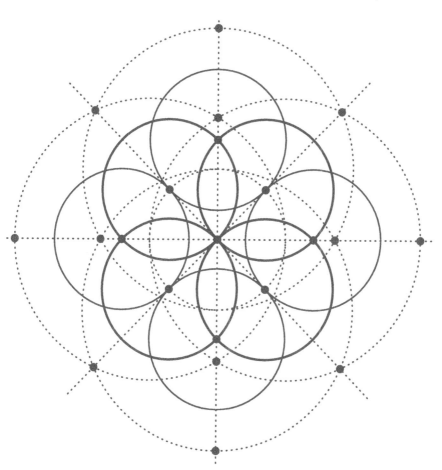

Sacred Geomrty

Focal Meditation

Breath & Focus on the center

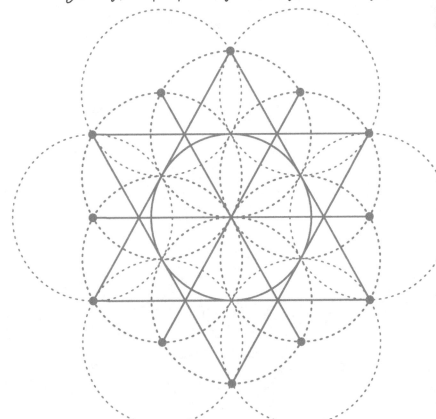

Sacred Geomrty

Focal Meditation

Breath & Focus on the center dot

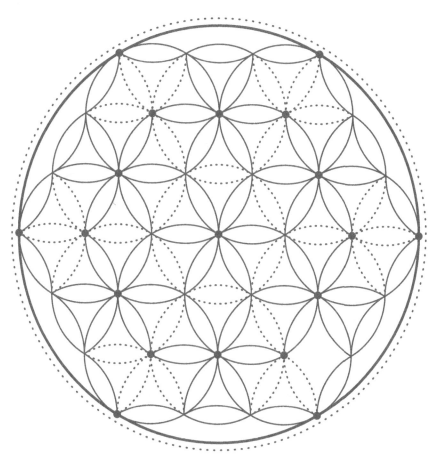

Meditative Coloring

Meditative Coloring

Meditative Coloring

Meditative Coloring

Meditative Coloring

Meditative Coloring

More Space for me to listen and journal the thought from my Inner Compass
What am I letting go of - worry. fear. frustration. anger. people. situations? Who
and What am I grateful for? What are my petitions? Where is my true North?
Have the courage to Dream Big!

_____

_____

_____

_____

_____

_____

_____

_____

_____

_____

_____

_____

_____

_____

_____

_____

_____

_____

"Believe. You're halfway there."

_____

_____

_____

_____

_____

_____

_____

_____

_____

_____

_____

_____

_____

_____

_____

_____

_____

_____

_____

Let your Inner Compass guide you

_____
_____
_____
_____
_____
_____
_____
_____
_____
_____
_____
_____
_____
_____
_____
_____
_____
_____
_____

Let your Inner Compass guide you

Let your Inner Compass guide you

Let your Inner Compass guide you

thank you!

Review

As a small business, I personally thank you in advance for your purchase! Please take 2 minutes and provide us with your 5* review! Please consider gifting this book to your friends and family! Maybe even make it a 30 day book club activity! Stay in touch! I love your feedback. Please check out my other books, yoga teacher trainings, events, and retreats!

@ericagarciayoga

EMAIL
erica@ericagarciayoga.com

WEB
www.ericagarciayoga.com

Made in the USA
Monee, IL
24 June 2024

60598714R00075